SINGER'S CHOICE

PROFESSIONAL TRACKS FOR SERIOUS SINGERS

Sing More Songs by

George & Ira Gershwin

2105

George Gershwin began working on Broadway musicals in 1916, contributing the music to 25 shows that were primarily written by other composers; all but two were from 1916-26. Most significantly, he was the chief composer for 31 other shows during 1919-35 with his brother Ira Gershwin being his main lyricist by 1924. Among the biggest successes for the Gershwins were Lady Be Good (from which came "Fascinatin' Rhythm"), Oh Kay (which debuted "Someone To Watch Over Me"), Strike Up The Band, Funny Face, Show Girl, Girl Crazy and Of Thee I Sing. Two of Gershwin's songs, "I Got Rhythm" and "Lady Be Good," utilized chord changes that became among the most common and popular in jazz. Gershwin, who could play very good stride piano, always admired the top jazz pianists and dozens of his songs were adopted and frequently recorded by jazz musicians in his lifetime.

If Gershwin had only written such popular songs for Broadway productions as "Somebody Loves Me," "The Man I Love" and "I've Got A Crush On You," he would still be famous today. But Gershwin was rarely content to stand still. In 1924 he composed "Rhapsody In Blue" for Paul Whiteman's orchestra. The piece was revolutionary in blending together the feeling of jazz, and a general bluesiness with classical music. At that point, jazz had rarely shared the stage much less a lengthy piece with classical music. Gershwin performed the classic work with Whiteman's band at its debut (improvising a few cadenzas that had not been fully written yet) and he appeared on the Rhapsody's first two recordings. Gershwin also composed such extended classical works as "Concerto In F," "An American In Paris," "Second Rhapsody" and "Cuban Overture."

In the early 1920s, Gershwin had written a one-act opera Blue Monday that was considered so far ahead of its time that it was only performed once during the era. In 1935 he wrote the first successful jazz/folk opera, "Porgy And Bess." The score included several songs that became standards, most notably "Summertime," "It Ain't Necessarily So" and "I Loves You Porgy."

Whether it was appearing as a host of a couple of radio series, writing for films, or performing in public, George Gershwin seemed to be everywhere during the 1930s. Throughout the last 20 years of his life, he was a whirlwind of activity, almost as if he knew that he only had a limited amount of time in which to achieve his life's work. He spent his last year in Hollywood, writing the music for the Fred Astaire films Shall We Dance (which included "Let's Call The Whole Thing Off" and "They Can't Take That Away From Me") and Damsel In Distress.

The world was shocked when, after a relatively short period of worsening health, George Gershwin died in 1937 from a brain tumor. He was just 38. One can only speculate as to the many great works (in both popular music and classical) that were never composed because of Gershwin's premature death. But looking at it the opposite way, one must be very thankful that Gershwin wrote so much. In his short life he composed such memorable songs as the cheerful "Bidin' My Time," the heartfelt love song "I've Got A Crush On You," the offbeat "But Not For Me" and the exuberant "S' Wonderful," not to mention the always tricky "Fascinatin' Rhythm." George Gershwin's musical legacy is so strong and his accomplishments so vast that he will always be rated as one of America's greatest composers.

Scott Yanow,
author of 11 books including Swing,
Jazz On Film and Jazz On Record 1917-76

Sing More Songs by

George & Ira Gershwin

CONTENTS

ISBN 978-1-941566-04-6

Of Thee I Sing

Words and Music by
Ira Gershwin and George Gershwin

Embraceable You

Words and Music by
Ira Gershwin and George Gershwin

MMO 2105

Oh, Lady Be Good

Words and Music by
Ira Gershwin and George Gershwin

How Long Has This Been Going On?

Words and Music by
Ira Gershwin and George Gershwin

MMO 2105

9

10

Summertime

Words and Music by
Ira Gershwin, Du Bose,
Dorothy Heyward, and George Gershwin

Lyrics:

Sum-mer - time___ and the li-vin' is eas - y;___ Fish are jump-in'___ and the cot-ton is high;___ Oh, your dad-dy's rich___ and your ma is good look - in';___ So hush lit-tle ba-by don't___ you cry.___

One of these morn-in's you're gon-na rise___ up sing - in';___ An you'll spread your wings and you'll take to the sky;___ But 'til that morn-in'___ there's a noth-in' can harm you;___ With dad - dy and mam-my stand in' by.___

Love Walked In

Words and Music by
Ira Gershwin and George Gershwin

53 G C   D⁷   G⁷   C   D⁷

One look and I for - got the gloom of the past; One look and I had found my fu-ture at

60 G⁷   C   F   Dmi⁷   Fmi

last; One look and I had found the world com - plete - ly

65 C   Dmi⁷   G⁷   C E♭   A♭ma⁷ D♭ma⁷ C⁶

new when love walked in with you._____

Nice Work If You Can Get It

Words and Music by
Ira Gershwin and George Gershwin

I Got Rhythm

Words and Music by
Ira Gershwin and George Gershwin

15

MMO 2105

MUSIC MINUS ONE
50 Executive Boulevard • Elmsford, New York 10523-1325
914-592-1188 • e-mail: info@musicminusone.com
www.musicminusone.com

MMO 2105

ISBN 978-1-941566-04-6